A New Tune A Day™

Performance Pieces
for Flute

Compiled and arranged by Ned Bennett

Chord symbols for all pieces are included for
guitar or keyboard accompaniment.

Boston Music Company
part of The Music Sales Group
London/New York/Paris/Sydney/Copenhagen/Berlin/Madrid/Tokyo

Contents

Published by

Boston Music Company

Exclusive Distributors:

Music Sales Corporation

257 Park Avenue South, New York, NY 10010, USA

Music Sales Limited

8/9 Frith Street, London W1D 3JB, UK

Music Sales Pty Limited

120 Rothschild Avenue, Rosebery, NSW 2018, Australia

This book © Copyright 2006 Boston Music Company, a division of Music Sales Corporation.

Compiled and edited by Ned Bennett

Series Editor: David Harrison

Music processed by Paul Ewers Music Design

Cover and book designed by Chloë Alexander

Photography by Matthew Ward

Printed in the US

Backing tracks by Guy Dagul

CD recorded, mixed and mastered by Jonas Persson and John Rose

Your Guarantee of Quality

As publishers, we strive to produce every book to the highest commercial standards. The music has been freshly engraved and the book has been carefully designed to minimize awkward page turns and to make playing from it a real pleasure. Throughout, the printing and binding have been planned to ensure a sturdy, attractive publication which should give years of enjoyment. If your copy fails to meet our high standards, please inform us and we will gladly replace it.

www.musicsales.com

Amazing Grace

Traditional

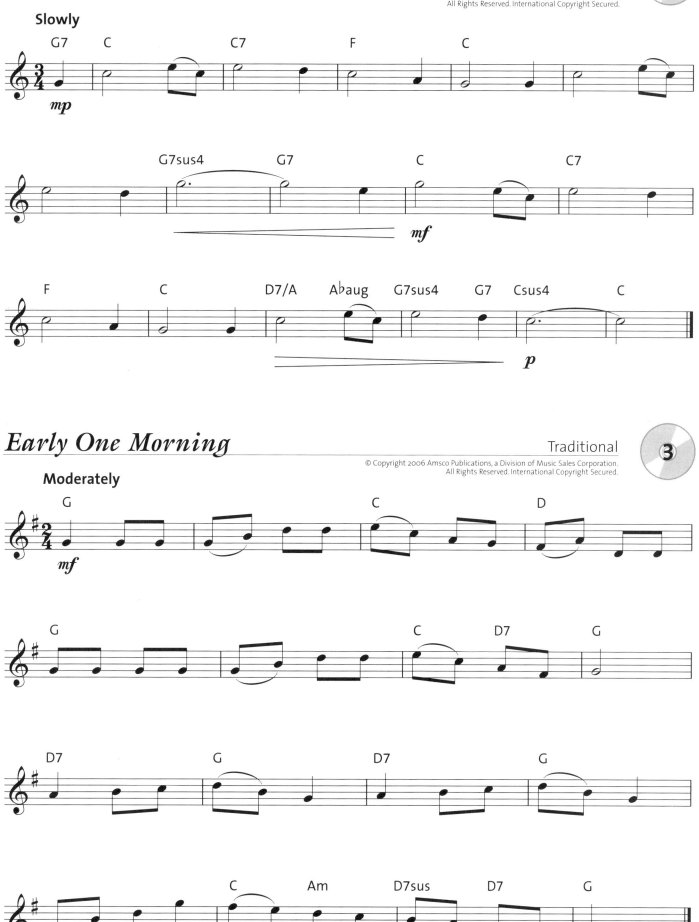

Early One Morning

Traditional

Santa Lucia

Neapolitan Traditional

© Copyright 2006 Amsco Publications, a Division of Music Sales Corporation.
All Rights Reserved. International Copyright Secured.

Moderately

Poor Little Buttercup (from HMS Pinafore)

Sullivan

© Copyright 2006 Amsco Publications, a Division of Music Sales Corporation.
All Rights Reserved. International Copyright Secured.

Gently

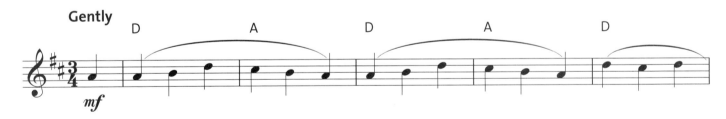

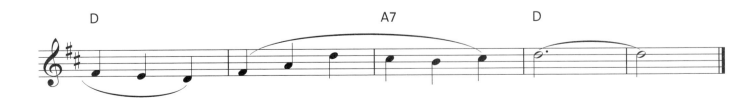

My Bonnie Lies Over The Ocean

Scottish Traditional

Lullaby

Brahms

Kalinka

Russian Traditional

© Copyright 2006 Amsco Publications, a Division of Music Sales Corporation.
All Rights Reserved. International Copyright Secured.

Moderato

Once In Royal David's City

Guantlett

© Copyright 2006 Amsco Publications, a Division of Music Sales Corporation.
All Rights Reserved. International Copyright Secured.

Moderato

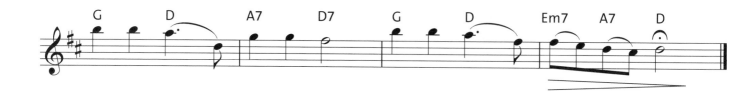

Molly Malone

Banana Boat Song

12 Telstar

Meek

Moderately quick

Satin Doll

Ellington, Strayhorn & Mercer

Moderate swing

14 *Coasts Of High Barbary*

American Traditional

Fairly quick

15 *Babu Sau*

Ngizim Traditional

Lively

Mama Don't Allow

American Traditional

16

Lively swing

La Cucaracha

Mexican Traditional

17

18 ## *Shenandoah*

19 ## *Turkey In The Straw*

Steal Away

Over The Hills

22 *Catch A Falling Star*

Vance & Pockriss

Moderate (Rumba)

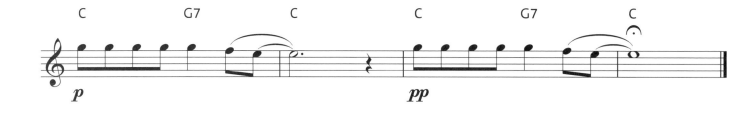

Underneath The Arches

McCarthy, Flannigan & Connely

24 Ding Dong Merrily On High

16th Century French

25 By The Rivers Of Babylon

Caribbean Traditional

Old Folks At Home

Minuet

Williams

Angel Eyes

Slow swing

30 *Dick's Maggot*

Scottish Traditional
© Copyright 2006 Amsco Publications, a Division of Music Sales Corporation.
All Rights Reserved. International Copyright Secured.

Moderately

31 *Nobody Knows*

Burleigh
© Copyright 2006 Amsco Publications, a Division of Music Sales Corporation.
All Rights Reserved. International Copyright Secured.

Slowly

British Grenadiers

Boldly

Minuet

Allegretto

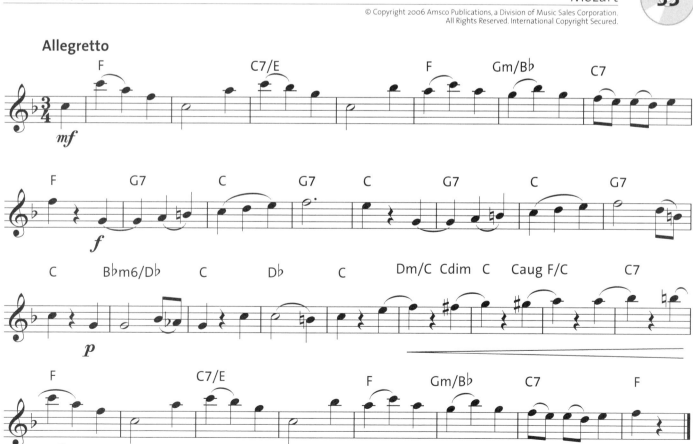

34 *Greensleeves*

 English Traditional

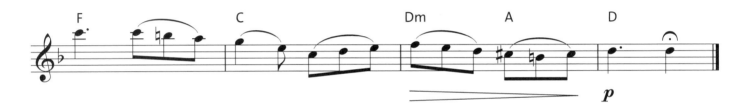

35 *The Hebrides Overture* (excerpt) Mendelssohn

The Keel Row

Scottish Traditional
© Copyright 2006 Amsco Publications, a Division of Music Sales Corporation.
All Rights Reserved. International Copyright Secured.

Brisk (optional swing)

Mexican Hat Dance

Mexican Traditional
© Copyright 2006 Amsco Publications, a Division of Music Sales Corporation.
All Rights Reserved. International Copyright Secured.

To Coda

D.S. al Coda — *Coda*

38 *Perdido*

Tizol

Swing

Blackadder Theme

Moderately

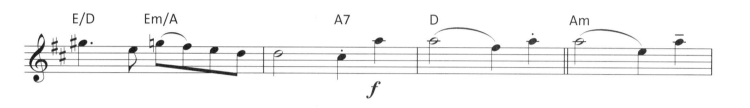

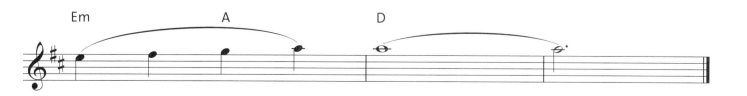

40 **Deep River**

41 **Das Wandern**

Hatikvah

Cohen

The Ash Grove

Welsh Traditional

44 Bill Bailey

American Traditional

Fast swing

45 Tit Willow (from *The Mikado*)

Sullivan

Moderato

Waltz

Brahms

46

Moderately

47 *Men Of Harlech* Welsh Traditional

Moderato

48 *Rock-A-My Soul* Spiritual

Moderate swing

Estampie

Lively

D and A throughout

We'll Meet Again

Parker & Charles

Moderate swing

Diamonds Are A Girl's Best Friend

Styne & Robin

51

Lively

52 Jeanie With The Light Brown Hair

Foster

Gently

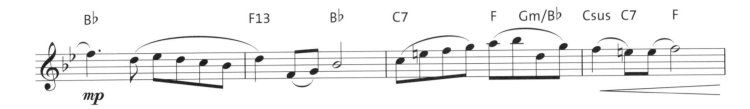

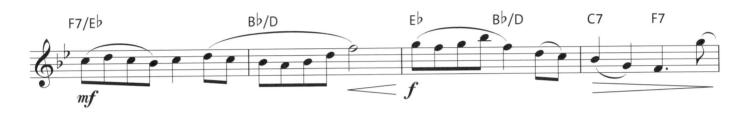

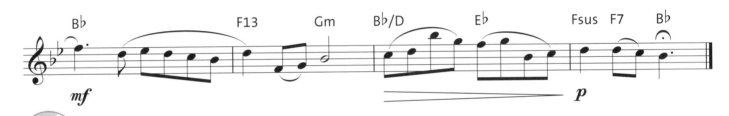

53 Emperor Quartet (excerpt)

Beethoven

Adagio

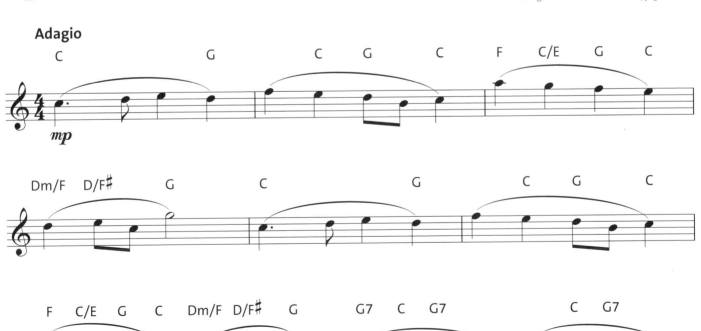

Swan Lake (excerpt)

Tchaikovsky

Andante cantabile

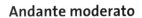

55 Polovtsian Dance

Borodin

Andante moderato

Dark Eyes

Russian Traditional

56

Jupiter (from *The Planets Suite*)

Holst

Andante

Bring Me Sunshine

Steady swing

59

The Frim Fram Sauce

Ricardel & Evans

Moderate swing

Try A Little Tenderness

Woods, Campbell & Connelly

60

Moderate swing

Grand March (from *Aida*)

Verdi

Boldly

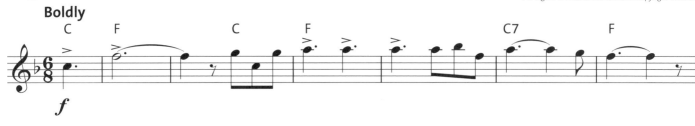

Radetsky March

Nellie The Elephant

Hart & Butler

Moderately

64 *John Brown's Body*

Medium swing

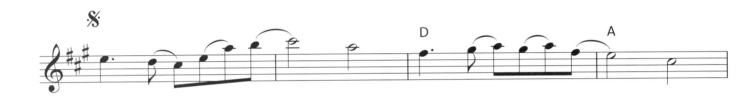

In The Hall Of The Mountain King (from *Peer Gynt*)   Grieg

Fig Leaf Rag   Joplin

CD backing tracks

1	Tuning Note	23	Underneath The Arches	45	Tit Willow
2	Amazing Grace	24	Ding Dong Merrily On High	46	Brahms Waltz
3	Early One Morning	25	By The Rivers Of Babylon	47	Men Of Harlech
4	Santa Lucia	26	Old Folks At Home	48	Rock-A-My Soul
5	Poor Little Buttercup	27	Bach Minuet	49	Estampie
6	My Bonnie Lies Over The Ocean	28	Jurassic Park Theme	50	We'll Meet Again
7	Lullaby	29	Angel Eyes	51	Diamonds Are A Girl's Best Friend
8	Kalinka	30	Dick's Maggot	52	Jeanie With The Light Brown Hair
9	Once In Royal David's City	31	Nobody Knows	53	Emperor Quartet
10	Molly Malone	32	British Grenadiers	54	Swan Lake
11	Banana Boat Song	33	Mozart Minuet	55	Polovtsian Dance
12	Telstar	34	Greensleeves	56	Dark Eyes
13	Satin Doll	35	The Hebrides Overture	57	Jupiter
14	Coasts Of High Barbary	36	The Keel Row	58	Bring Me Sunshine
15	Babu Sau	37	Mexican Hat Dance	59	The Frim Fram Sauce
16	Mama Don't Allow	38	Perdido	60	Try A Little Tenderness
17	La Cucaracha	39	Blackadder Theme	61	Grand March
18	Shenandoah	40	Deep River	62	Radetsky March
19	Turkey In The Straw	41	Das Wandern	63	Nellie The Elephant
20	Steal Away	42	Hatikvah	64	John Brown's Body
21	Over The Hills	43	The Ash Grove	65	In The Hall Of The Mountain King
22	Catch A Falling Star	44	Bill Bailey	66	Fig Leaf Rag

How to use the CD

The tuning note on track 1 is A.

After track 1, the backing tracks are listed in the order in which they appear in the book. Look for the symbol in the book for the relevant backing track.

Listen for the clicks at the start of each track: depending on the tempo and time signature, each track will have clicks for one or two bars before the melody begins. When the melody starts with an anacrusis, the click will also play for the first part of the bar.